Aloha,

My name is Lahela Chandler Correa. I was born and raised (on) Kaua'i in the Wainiha Valley. Two miles from where I lived (was an) acre kalo (taro) field which provided food for ourselves and (others).

My parents Francis Sr. and Kapeka Chandler were born and (raised) both came from a large 'ohana (family). In my immediate family I have 10 brothers, 5 sisters and one half sister. I am number 13 of all my siblings.

Both my parents were great examples of Aloha. They showed us "Aloha" by living it every day. They taught us that Aloha was taking care of your family, being kind to everyone, being helpful, being honest, always setting a good example, working hard, doing your best, keeping our name good and always respecting your elders.

For me "Aloha" is not just a word, it has a deeper meaning that is endless. Like all things in life if not passed down and taught, it will be forgotten.

Aloha is a way of life that was taught for generations to our people. This is who we are, we live it, we breath it every day of our lives. This is how the first foreigners were greeted when they came here. Aloha means that when we meet someone they are greeted with utmost kindness. When we offer to do something, nothing is expected in return and when we share we give freely.

It doesn't matter if you are white, black, blue or green, I believe we all have "Aloha". Aloha is considered the gift of the Hawaiian people to the world. Learn and share Aloha today.

Aloha,
Lahela

Lahela's lineage stretches across and touches many islands.

Her father Francis's genealogy comes from Maui and Kaua'i. His ancestors, the Kanialamas, were the genealogists and attendants to Queen Emma and her family. The families were one of the early migrators from Tahiti and whose offspring eventually settled on Kaua'i and set roots in Kahili near Kīlauea, Kaua'i.

Her Mother Elizabeth comes from the Mahuiki and 'Īlālā'ole lines from Hā'ena, Kaua'i and Puna on Hawai'i Island respectively. The Mahuiki Family is famous for their knowledge of fishing in the Hā'ena area.

The 'Īlālā'oles are from Puna and are descendants of Kamehameha I.

This book belongs to:_____

My Hawaiian name is:_____

Hawai'i is a very special place that is strong in its culture, traditions and language.

The core of the Hawaiian culture is 'ohana.

Aloha – "What it Means to my 'Ohana and Yours" supports these values.

Aloha is Akua

Aloha is Love

Aloha is a Greeting

Aloha is Kuleana

Aloha is Mana

Aloha is Malama

Aloha is Respect

Aloha is Hope

Aloha is Light

Aloha is Kokua

Aloha is Kindness

Aloha is Pono

Aloha is Openness

Aloha is Sharing

The Hawaiian Flag - Read, Learn and Color

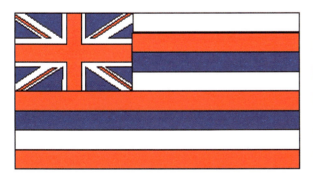

In 1810 Kamehameha I was the first king to rule all of the Hawaiian Islands. He was born of Hawaiian royalty and became known as Kamehameha the Great. Around 1816, Kamehameha created his own flag which was a combination of the British and United States flag to help keep peace and avoid any problems. In about 1845 his flag was altered and was adopted as the Hawaiian State Flag as shown on this page.

The upper left hand corner of the flag is inspired by the flag of Great Britain and the stripes were inspired by the United States Flag. Each of the eight stripes of red, white and blue represent the islands of Hawaii as follows: Hawaiʻi, Oʻahu, Kauaʻi, Kahoʻolawe, Lānaʻi, Maui, Molokaʻi and Niʻihau.

HAWAIIAN ISLANDS

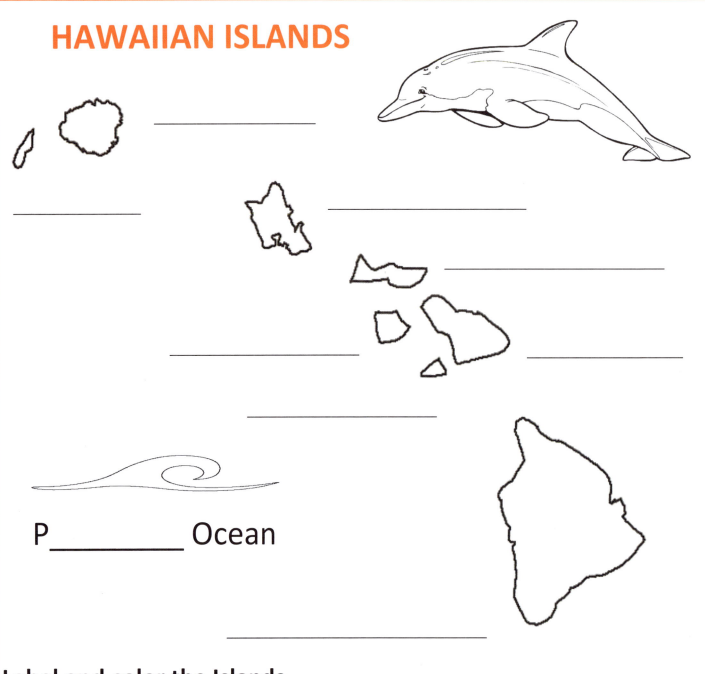

P_____ Ocean

Label and color the Islands

Hawaiʻi Island - ʻUlaʻula (red)
Kauaʻi - Poni (purple)
Niʻihau – Polū (light blue)
Kahoʻolawe - ʻĀhinahina (gray)

Oʻahu - Melemele (yellow)
Maui - ʻAkala (pink)
Lānaʻi - ʻAlani (orange)
Molokaʻi - ʻŌmaʻomaʻo (green)

Did you know?? On May 1 in Hawaiʻi, we celebrate May Day which is Lei Day. The celebration consists of many festivities. There is a royal court procession, part of which are eight princesses that represent each island, dressed in their island's color and lei. The lei's are made from each islands chosen flower or shell. Many schools celebrate with hula and other cultural events.

The Hawaiian Islands were formed by volcanoes. The earth is made up of giant slabs. As these slabs move on the bottom of the ocean floor they travel over areas called hotspots. These hotspots act like a hot blowtorch that turns the rocks into a liquid substance called magma. As seen in the picture, the magma rises up through the pipe and erupts, shooting out hot lava. When magma erupts out of the volcano it is then called lava. When the lava cools it turns into volcanic rock. This continuous eruption is how the Hawaiian Islands were all formed. As the slab moves off the hot spot, it slowly moves the island formed, until a new island forms above the hot spot. The island of Hawai'i, also known as the Big Island is now on top of the hotspot that Kaua'i was on 4.5 million years ago. Therefore, Kaua'i is the oldest island.

The island of O'ahu was formed about 3 million years ago. Moloka'i was formed about 1.8 million years ago and Maui is a little less than a million years old.

There are currently 5 active volcanos in Hawai'i. On the Big Island there are Mauna Loa, Kīlauea, Hualālai and, one still under water and growing is Lō'ihi. Haleakalā on Maui is still considered an active volcano.

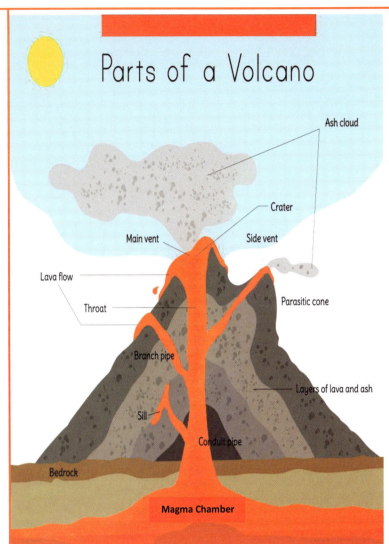

Color your new island and give it a name.
_____

 # ALOHA is Akua

This means Spirituality; inner peace. Like saying a **pule** (prayer; message of good wishes) before paddling a **wa'a** (outrigger canoe) in a race. This is a tradition in the **Hawaiian culture**. The **pule** can be two people or two hundred people all closing their eyes and holding hands as the head **kupuna** (elder) shares her/his **maika'i** (good) wishes and safety for all the paddlers.
What do you think?

Now close your eyes for a minute. Relax and find a quiet place inside yourself.

Write what you feel:_____

_____

_____

✏ Draw a picture of a place that makes you feel safe or peaceful:

[ ]

'Ohana Time: Create a pule at home with your 'ohana.

Approximately 2000 years ago, waʻa (outrigger canoes) brought the first Polynesians to the Hawaiian Islands and to this day are a very important part of the history and culture.

The first Polynesians traveled thousands of miles over the Pacific Ocean through stormy seas and howling winds. Their waʻa (canoes) were larger, some holding up to 80 people and were powered by sails. The waʻa were loaded with food, plants and animals to help them survive the voyage. They also brought seeds and seedlings to plant in their new home.

As time went on, some of the waʻa (canoes) became smaller and were used for fishing and a way to carry people and goods around the islands.

Native Hawaiians also used giant Koa trees from Hawaiʻi Island to make waʻa. Because the trees were so large, they could carve an entire waʻa from one tree.

Today waʻa (outrigger canoes) are used primarily for racing throughout the Hawaiian Islands. There are over 60 clubs throughout the islands promoting the sport, culture and tradition.

There is a deep love, respect and connection with the ocean and the Hawaiian people.

Did you know?? Outrigger canoeing is the official state team sport of Hawaiʻi.

The waʻa (outrigger canoe) has 6 noho (seats). The stroker sits in the front seat and is responsible for setting the pace. The steersperson sits in the back, steers the canoe, and is the captain.

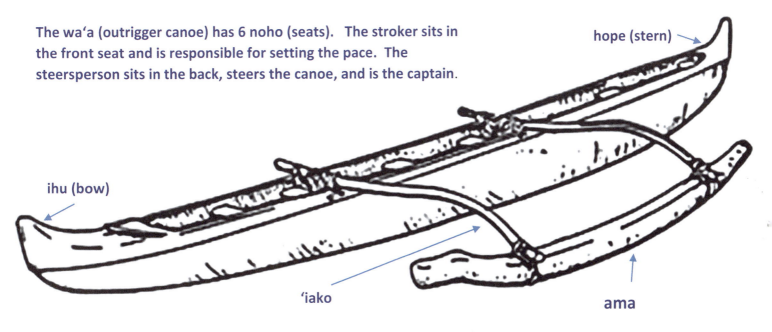

ihu (bow)

ʻiako

ama

hope (stern)

ALOHA is Love

American Sign Language for Love

Aloha means unconditional love in the Hawaiian language. This means we love someone the same, no matter if they are happy or sad. Always be forgiving and patient if they make a mistake. We not only say we love someone, we also show them through our actions.

Such as love like a mother or father hugging their kamaliʻi (children) or a keiki (child) hugging their pet showing their love.

What do you think?

We can never love too many people. In the hearts below list the names of people and ways you can show love.

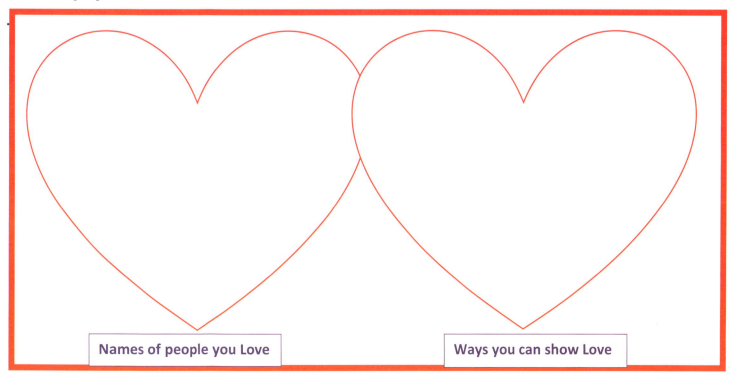

| Names of people you Love | Ways you can show Love |

ʻOhana Time – **In the back of the book, clip out the coupon book with 3 vouchers and staple.** Fill it out and give to someone in your ʻohana. Example: Good for one hug. (In back of book)

 # ALOHA is a Greeting

This is important as to how you say hello or goodbye. It must be said with true **Aloha** from the **puʻuwai** (heart).

Like giving someone a "**shaka**" (Hawaiian hand gesture to show **Aloha**) with a big **minoʻaka** (smile) on your face. In Hawaiʻi we also give a **pūliki** (hug) and **honi** (kiss) on the cheek to say **Aloha** (hello).

All cultures have their own word to say Hello; see if you can match these:

Word for Hello in a different language	Name of the Language
Bonjour	Italian
Konnichiwa	Hawaiian
Ciao	Filipino
Aloha	Japanese
Habari	Hindi
Hola	Spanish
Namaste	French
Kumusta	Swahili

What do you think?
Name/discuss another way you can greet or say hello to someone:
_____

 Make a Lei and greet a friend - Instructions on the next page.

ʻOhana Time - Make a lei with your ʻohana and present it to a loved one.

How To Make a Lei

Supplies you need to make homemade Hawaiian Leis:
- Colored cardstock or construction paper to cutout flowers
- Dried pasta noodles
- Drinking straws cut into 1 inch pieces
- Paper hole punch
- Colored yarn or thick String
- Floss threader

Directions – Start by cutting your flowers out and use the hole punch to put a hole in the middle of your paper flowers.
Cut the drinking straws into 1" pieces.
Cut your yarn or string into the length for your lei and tie onto the floss threader. Usually about 20" – 24" in length.
Start threading the flowers, pasta noodles and straws in any pattern you like. (Hint- use different colors of flowers to make your lei brighter.)
When finished tie the ends together and you have your lei!!

Presenting a Lei

Approach the person making eye contact and a smile. Put the lei over their head onto their shoulders, positioning it with half hanging in the front and half hanging in the back. Give them a nice **pūliki** (hug) and a **honi** (kiss) on the cheek passing on the **Aloha** to the person receiving the lei.

ALOHA is a Greeting

Pū, pronounced 'poo' is the Hawaiian name for the Conch Shell.

It is considered a gift from the **kai** (ocean) and its sound can travel very long distances.
The blowing of the **Pū** is used for many ceremonies and is a very important part of the Hawaiian culture.
It can have different meanings depending upon how many times it is blown, when it is blown and in which direction it is blown. These meanings are very sacred.

Long ago, the blowing of the **Pū** was a way for people to communicate between canoes, across the **kai** (ocean) and to those on the **'āina** (land). Sometimes it was used to request permission to come to shore. Permission or denial would then be returned from those on shore by them blowing the **Pū** (conch shell) back with a certain number of blows.
Today some people blow the **Pū** to say **Aloha** (Goodbye) at sunset to end the day and to say **Mahalo** (thanks).

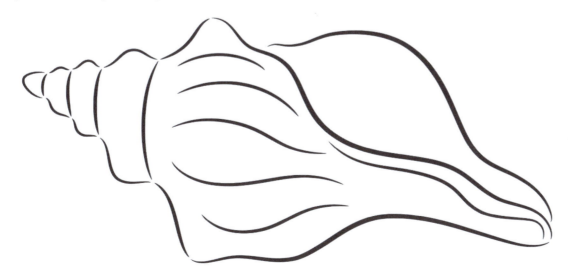

ALOHA is Kuleana

This means responsibility – everyone's responsibility. We accept our **kuleana** with honor and gratitude.

While sitting under the **ʻulu** (breadfruit tree), the **kumu** (teacher) teaches **kamaliʻi** (children) all about **Aloha**, culture and tradition and why it is important. Always remember **Aloha**.

What do you think?

What is the **Kumu's kuleana** ? _____

What is the **kuleana** of the **kamaliʻi** (children)? _____

Culture is: Draw a line to match the word on the left with the example listed on the right.

Food	Muʻumuʻu
Language – "Thank You"	Kamehmeha Day
Holiday	Lau hala Basket
Clothing	Leave slippers outside
Dance	Mahalo
Tradition	Poi
Art	Hula

Why is tradition important

#1._____

#2._____

Name two things that are your **kuleana** at home?

#1._____

#2._____

ʻOhana Time – Write down one tradition you have at home with your ʻohana.

ALOHA is Mana

This means good or positive energy that can come from a place, person, thing or idea. It fills you up and makes you feel **maika'i** (good) inside. Like sunbeams shining down, warming you up on a beautiful sandy **kahakai** (beach) in **Hawai'i**. What do you think?

Write one word that *tells how you feel* when you see:

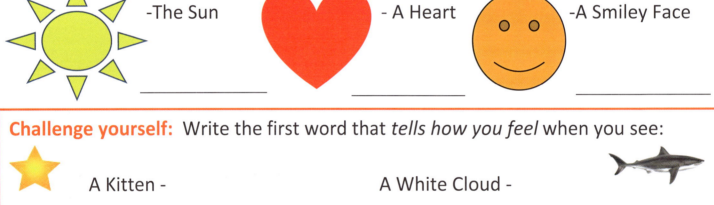

- The Sun _____
- A Heart _____
- A Smiley Face _____

Challenge yourself: Write the first word that *tells how you feel* when you see:

A Kitten -

A **Hōkū** *(star)* -

A **Honu** *(turtle)* -

A Flash of lightning -

A White Cloud -

A **Manō** *(shark)* -

A **Hoaloha** *(friend)* -

A Balloon -

*Finish the sentence by filling in the blanks: _____ is such a great person because _____ always has something _____ to say about everyone and always tries their best to be _____.

*Name a place that makes you feel good inside_____.

'Ohana Time - At home make a list of all your 'ohana members and then ask them to write one thing they do to be positive people.

 # ALOHA is Malama

This means to care for all things; like the **aina** (land), your **'ohana** (family), yourself and all living creatures.

Such as, helping free a **honu** (turtle) that is tangled up in plastic, from garbage in the **kai** (ocean). Make sure when you're in the **kai,** you don't stand on the reef. It can kill the corals which are made up of many living organisms and home to many **i'a** (fish). What do you think?

List 3 things you do to take care of:

Yourself	'Āina (land)
#1. _____	#1. _____
#2. _____	#2. _____
#3. _____	#3. _____

Help Take Care of Our WORLD

Did you know?? Hundreds of thousands of honu, whales, and other marine mammals, and more than 1 million seabirds die each year from ocean pollution and ingestion or entanglement in marine debris. Marine debris is garbage thrown into the ocean.   http://www.seeturtles.org/ocean-plastic

Draw a picture of an animal you would save: example – Hawaiian Monk Seal

'Ohana Time - Write one way you would care for your 'ohana._____

ALOHA is Respect

This means showing honor or regard to people, places, things, and ideas.

In **Hawai'i** we greet **kūpuna** (elders) as Auntie or Uncle. When entering a **hale** (house) always leave your slippers outside the door. When visiting a **heiau** (sacred site) be careful of where you walk and do not remove or damage anything.

What do you think?

Read each sentence and circle the word that applies -Respectful or Disrespectful:

Hey can you give me those books.   **Respectful** or **Disrespectful**

Excuse me, do you know where the library is located? **Respectful** or **Disrespectful**

Interrupting someone when they are speaking. **Respectful** or **Disrespectful**

Texting on your phone at the dinner table. **Respectful** or **Disrespectful**

Thanks so much for the birthday presents.   **Respectful** or **Disrespectful**

Using your friends' bike without their permission.   **Respectful** or **Disrespectful**

Can you please help me with my homework? **Respectful** or **Disrespectful**

Write the name of a person you respect-_____

Finish the sentence: I respect her/him because they_____
_____.

Manners- fill in the blank letter: #1. P_ease   #2. _hank yo_   #3. E_cu_e m_

Why should we use manners? _____
_____

'Ohana Time - Discuss with your family how you show respect for each other.
Idea - Not to use cell phones at the dinner table. Write down one of your ideas:
_____

ALOHA is Hope

This means seeking and striving for **maikaʻi** (good) in all things. Hope is never giving up. Such as, a world of **maluhia** (peace) without fighting and wars. A world of love without hate. **A world full of Aloha.** What do you think?

If you think it, you can make it happen!

What would you change in the world to make it a better place:
Such as, a world of_____ ; without_____

*Draw a line to the word that means the opposite of the word in column 1.

Column 1	Column 2
healthy	mean
work	hate
kindness	illness
love	steal

Name one thing you would never give up on:_____

✎ Draw how you would write "**Aloha is Hope**" on your wall:

[   ]

ʻOhana Time- Discuss with your ʻohana and decide together on something you would like to improve.
My ʻohana can improve on_____.

Aloha Book Words

```
S U E I K K A Ē K E A A A A K A M M A L
A N U P U K A H A K A I A ' H I H L Ī E
P O E O A U Ō I A S A ' Ā O H E Ō A U U
A H A N A A K K A K H I L H N K A I U A
P Ō L O K A I U U A N A M A N Ō K M E U
Ō W O K N U O E L A H W K N L I P P Ā N
N L A Ē N H M Ā L A M A N A E L U K L K
H U K L U I H U M A L H Ō K Ū L E ' A Ī
I H A L U ' H Ē L K H N Ū U E A Ō A H H
P I A O P A H I A L A K ' A A N K U O K
```

WORD LIST:

ʻĀINA	HULA	KUMU	ʻOHANA
AKUA	KAHAKAI	KUPUNA	PONO
ALOHA	KAI	LEI	PULE
HALE	KEIKI	MAHALO	SHAKA
HAWAIʻI	KŌKUA	MĀLAMA	
HŌKŪLEʻA	KULA	MANA	
HONU	KULEANA	MANŌ	

Aloha Publishing Hawaii 2017

Hawaiian Foods

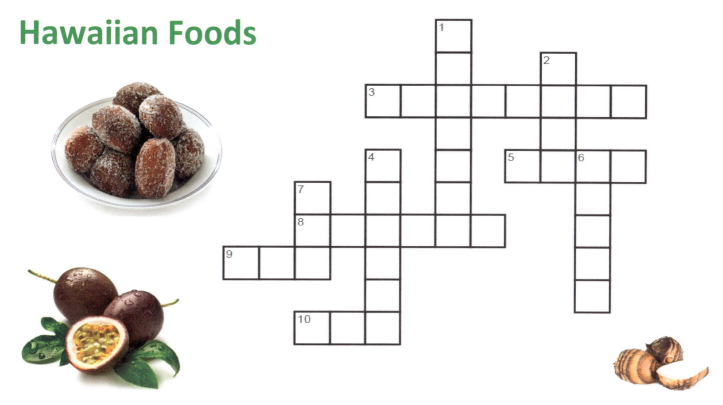

Across

3 Sugar covered chewy dough
5 A dish with chunks of raw fish, onions, salt, limu and sauce
8 Coconut Cream pudding
9 Thick paste made from taro
10 Underground oven to cook pork

Down

1 Passion fruit
2 Hawaiian word for taro
4 Chicken wrapped in ti leaves
6 _ _ _ _ _ pig
7 Yellowfin Tuna

WORD LIST:

AHI	KALO	LILIKOI	POKE
HAUPIA	KALUA	MALASADA	
IMU	LAULAU	POI	

Kalo also known as taro in English is a very important part of the Hawaiian culture and food source. Every part of the kalo plant can be eaten. The corm which is the bulb underground is eaten like potatoes or can be pounded into poi. The leaves taste like spinach and contain many vitamins. Kalo can be grown in marshy irrigated wetland patches (similar to rice paddies) and also in dry soil. As the Kalo plant gets older, it creates offshoots called 'ohā. As the shoots grow they will become full grown kalo plants and continue the growing cycle. As the 'ohā grows it multiplies and becomes a family of many kalo, which is where the word 'ohana comes from.

"The Hōkūleʻa – Voyaging Canoe"

The Hawaiian people have a very strong relationship with the ocean and a love for exploration. The voyaging vessel "The Hōkūleʻa meaning the "Star of Gladness" is a tribute to the Hawaiian culture past and present.

The Hōkūleʻa is a replication of the original canoes that brought the Polynesians to the islands of Hawaii approximately 2000 years ago. These canoes had disappeared and became extinct about 600 years ago, until an artist by the name of Herb Kane envisioned rebuilding these canoes used by his ancient ancestors.

He assembled a group of people from many different backgrounds to make this vision a reality. The Hōkūleʻa was built in 1970 and had its first successful voyage to Tahiti in 1976. When they arrived in Tahiti, 17,000 people cheered them into shore. The Tahitians shared this love for voyaging canoes, navigators and tradition.

The Hōkūleʻa is not motorized, has no engine or modern day electronics or gadgets to guide her to her destination. The Hōkūleʻa is driven by the sails and the winds of the seas. She is guided lovingly by the ancient system of navigating by the stars. The original navigator was a man by the name of Mau Piailug from the small island of Satawai in Micronesia, who then trained Nainoa Thompson to carry on this great navigating tradition.

For the past 41 years the Hōkūleʻa has traveled and explored the oceans across the globe. To follow the travels of the Hōkūleʻa please visit their website at www.hokulea.com. Learn more about this incredible voyaging canoe and her adventures and the brave men and women that have kept navigating by the stars alive for all future generations to admire and appreciate.

It is our honor at Aloha Movement Kauai to encourage everyone to read about the Hōkūleʻa and appreciate her courage and keep the tradition of this great voyaging canoe alive.

Mahalo Nui for your inspiration and perseverance.

What would you name your Voyaging Canoe?

_____

We would like to recognize all the crew that have sailed and helped on the Hōkūle'a - one of our 'ohana had the privilege.
Aloysius Kahimoku Pu`ulei-Chandler aka Moku Boy

Ho'okele wa'a (navigator)

Hōkūle'a
Star of Gladness

On a recent voyage he was one of 12 Crew Members, both men and women. Some of the jobs of the crew members include kapena (captain), doctor, cook, steersman, safety man, media person, navigator and educators. They all have great respect and passion for their journey. Moku had the honor to crew on the Hōkūle'a from South Africa, Brazil, Easter Island, Pitcairn Island, and Marquesas to Tahiti.

 # ALOHA is Light

This means living a life of goodness. Always choose the path of **maikaʻi** (good) over bad. Live, talk and act from a **puʻuwai** (heart) full of **Aloha**.
Like standing up for someone that is being bullied and how it makes you feel **maikaʻi** (good); just like looking at a beautiful **ānuenue** (rainbow).
If someone was being made fun of, what would you do?
_____

Listed below are choices. Circle the good choices in **Blue** and the bad choices in **Orange**.
#1. Working hard for your money.
#2. Sneaking out of the **hale** (house) when you are grounded.
#3. Whispering about someone behind their back.
#4. Returning a wallet full of money that you found on the ground.
#5. Copying someone's homework because you forgot to do it.

Color your ānuenue (rainbow) below with any colors you want. Get really creative!!

ALOHA is KŌKUA

This means giving of yourself to **kōkua** (help) others and make the world a better place. Like **kamaliʻi** (children) helping deliver food in the "**Aloha Food Truck**", to people in their community so they don't go **pōloli** (hungry). What do you think?

Make a list of things you can do in your school and community to help others:

Kula (School) List

1._____
2._____
3._____

Community List

1._____
2._____
3._____

Write a story about how you would help someone, using the words in the Word Bank:

| Word Bank: | help | friend | give | three | red |

_____
_____
_____
_____
_____
_____
_____

ʻOhana Time: Write down a way you and your ʻohana can kōkua to make the world a better place! _____

Did you know

Hawaiʻi is known for its sweet **hala kahiki** (pineapple) and acres of pineapple fields throughout the islands. But the pineapple is not originally from the islands. It is believed to have first arrived on Hawaiʻi in the early to mid-1500.

Each plant must be planted by hand in the field. A good planter can plant up to 10,000 pineapple crowns a day. The plant is the crown top with green leaves.

It takes almost 2 years for a plant to bear its first pineapple and about another 15 months for the second fruit. That just goes to show that some things are worth waiting for.

HALA TREE

Not only do we give of ourselves to kōkua, but so does the world around us. A perfect example is the Hala, which is a native tree of Hawaiʻi.

The leaves of the Hala are called lau (meaning leaf) hala, which are long and twisted with sharp edges. When dried and stripped they can are woven by weavers into many items such as mats, bracelets, hats, bags and fan. They were also used for thatching roofs.

The female tree bears a fruit that looks similar to a pineapple. When the fruit falls on the ground it breaks up into little pieces called keys. When they dry they can be used as paint brushes.

The first Polynesians also brought Hala, which they used to weave the sails for their canoes.

ALOHA is Kindness

This means showing compassion, caring and generosity from the **puʻuwai** (heart). Treating everyone with kindness and being an **ʻoluʻolu** (nice) person.

Like when you are out surfing with your **hoaloha** (friend) and letting them get the set wave (best wave).

What do you think?

Make a **Kindness Pledge** for yourself. Fill in the blank (example: a hug)

Every day, I promise to be kind to everyone by greeting them with a smile and _____.

Fill in the sentences with 3 different ways you can be kind to your friends.

#1. I will help my friends_____.

#2. I tell my friends_____.

#3. I share _____with my friends.

Aloha Kindness Package: The next time someone does something nice, thank them by making a kindness package. In the back of the book you will find 2 wrappers you can cut out and use or make your own like the one below and color. Take the wrapper put a piece of candy or small gift and wrap it up, tie the ends with a 10" ribbon and tape the back closed.

ALOHA

"Mahalo or Thank You"
For Being Such a Nice Person!

ʻOhana Time - Do something that is really kind for one of your ʻohana and then ask them to do something really kind for someone else and keep passing on a kind deed.

ALOHA is Pono

This means living with integrity and having **maikaʻi** (good) morals and values. Living a good **kūpono** (honest) **ola** (life).

Living your **ola** (life) with peace and fairness with everyone and in everything you do. Do the right thing and make good decisions in your **ola** (life). A good way to practice is to always do what's right even when no one is looking. Like when you are walking on the **kahakai** (beach) and pick up **ʻōpala** (trash) instead of leaving it on the ground. What do you think?

Good morals and values. Always be **Pono.**

#1. -You have a test at school and someone gives you the answers to the test. It would be easy to use the answers, but you know it's not right and decide to do it on your own. By doing this you are being **honest**. (write the word in the star).

#2. – You get really mad at your friend for breaking your favorite skateboard. You find out later that it was an accident and feel bad about getting so upset, so you go to your friend and apologize for getting so mad. It takes **courage** to apologize. (write the word in the star)

#3. – Your Dad asks you to mow the lawn, when your friends come by and ask you to go play a game of soccer. You are really tempted to go play and mow the lawn later, but decide to stay and do as your Dad asked. By doing this you are being **responsible**. (write the word in the star)

All the examples above show us how to live a Pono life. Listed below are a few more ways to live Pono. See if you can unscramble these words and practice them in your life:

ienc _ _ _ _   cpetrse _ _ _ _ _ _ _   velo _ _ _ _   tsurt _ _ _ _ _   gvnigi _ _ _ _ _ _

ʻOhana Time - **Draw a Heart and cut it out, then write "I love you" on it. Surprise them by taping it on the bathroom mirror.**

 # ALOHA is Openness

This means to accept people or things as they are and not be judgmental. Don't make a decision about someone, without getting to know them. Treat others as you want to be treated. Like being 'olu'olu (nice) to a new kid in kula (school) or in the neighborhood even if they look, talk or dress differently than you. Aloha does not discriminate.   What do you think?

Name 2 things you can do to make someone feel welcome at school?

#1._____

#2._____

People dress differently in some countries. Draw a line between the type of clothing on the left and the country with its flag on the right.

Sari (wrap)   Scotland

Mu'umu'u (Dress)   Japan

Kilt (skirt)   India

Flamenco Dress   Alaska

Kimono (robe)   Spain

Mukluk (winter boot)   Hawaii

_____

Have you ever been the new kids in school, in a sport, in a group of friends or in the neighborhood? If so, which one?_____

How did it make you feel?_____

_____

ALOHA is Openness

On the previous page there is a message drawn in the sand "Friends Forever". What message would you draw in the sand? Draw it below.

Aloha for Everyone

#1. Do these people all look the same? Circle an answer and why: YES   NO   CAN'T TELL

Why?_____

#2. Do they all think the same? Circle an answer and why: YES   NO   CAN'T TELL

Why?_____

#3. Should they be treated the same? Circle an answer and why: YES   NO   CAN'T TELL

Why?_____

ALOHA
Is Openness

Create Your Ānuenue (Rainbow)

A blind person may not be able to see a rainbow the way people with sight do, so they use their other senses to see the world around them. Your rainbow will be made of different textures which will represent the different colors of the rainbow. This allows a blind person to create a picture of it in their mind by seeing it through their touch.

<u>Materials Needed:</u>

Rainbow Template
Cardboard
Glue
Cut up straws
Elbow Macaroni
Cotton balls
Flat Buttons
Sequins
Pom Poms
Uncooked Lima or Kidney beans

<u>Directions</u>

#1. Use your Rainbow Template in the back of the book. Cut out the page and copy. Then glue it on a piece of cardboard and start creating.

#2. On the "Red" band, glue down the elbow macaroni all the way across the band. Place the macaroni any way you would like, as long as it fits in the band. Remember to glue all pieces across the whole band.

#3. On the "Orange" band, glue down flat plastic buttons.

#4. On the "Yellow" band, glue down the pom poms.

#5. On the "Green" band, glue down the pieces of straws. You will need to cut your straws into ½ inch pieces before you can glue them down. Glue the straws down across the whole band.

#6. On the "Blue" band, glue down the cotton balls.

#7. On the "Indigo" (dark blue) band, glue down the beans.

#8. On the "Violet" band, glue down the sequins.

Congratulations – you have completed your rainbow. Now take your rainbow, close your eyes and run your finger slowly over the top and feel the different textures and shapes. This is how a blind person sees the different colors in their mind.

ALOHA is Sharing

This means living your **ola** (life) without greed. If you have more than you need, then share with others. Share **Aloha** every day. Like when you go fishing, feed your **'ohana** (family), then share the rest of the **i'a** (fish) you catch with your **hoaloha** (friend).
What do you think?

You are given three $20.00 bills to share.
Write down who gets each bill and why.
For yours, write down what you would do with the money.

You (name)_____   What_____

Anyone (who)_____   Why_____

Donate (who)_____   Why_____

Yellowfin Tuna is known as **'Ahi** in Hawai'i. The **'Ahi** is one of the larger tuna species and can weigh up to 400 pounds (400 lbs.)

Question? If you catch a 100 lb. **'Ahi** and give each family 10 pounds of fish to eat, **how many families could you feed?** _____

Challenge Question – If you catch a 400 lb. **'Ahi**, how many families could you feed? _____

Did you know?
The state fish of Hawai'i is Humuhumunukunukuāpua'a

'Ohana Time -Talk with your 'ohana and discuss what you can do to share with others. It may be a donation to a charity or maybe taking extra clothes you no longer need and sharing with a family in need.

Draw your own fish on the next page.

How many big fish are in the picture?_____

How many small fish are in the picture?_____

How many fish are there altogether? _____

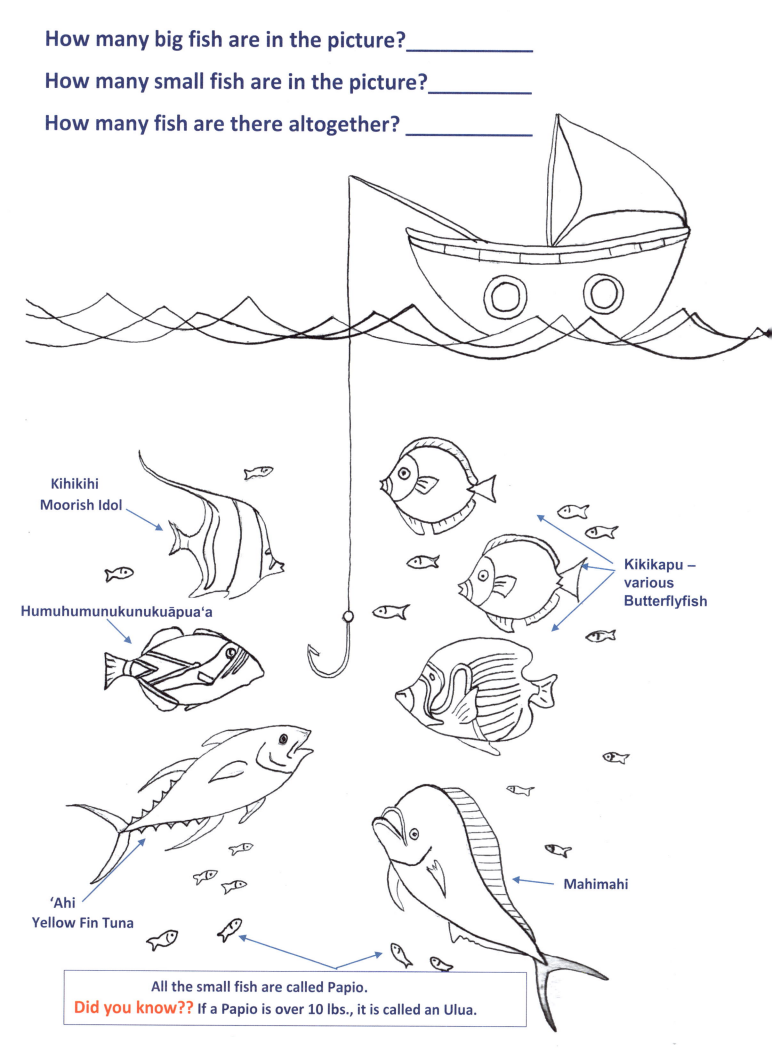

Kihikihi Moorish Idol

Humuhumunukunukuāpuaʻa

Kikikapu – various Butterflyfish

Mahimahi

ʻAhi Yellow Fin Tuna

All the small fish are called Papio.
Did you know?? If a Papio is over 10 lbs., it is called an Ulua.

Hula is the physical embodiment of prayer. It expresses the feelings and emotions of what we experience in our everyday life and while in its grips allows us to be in touch with the divine. Every movement, expression and gesture in hula has a specific meaning. It represent plants, animals, and the world around us.

From the Kai (Ocean) of words below, match the English words with the Hawaiian word and write it in the circle.

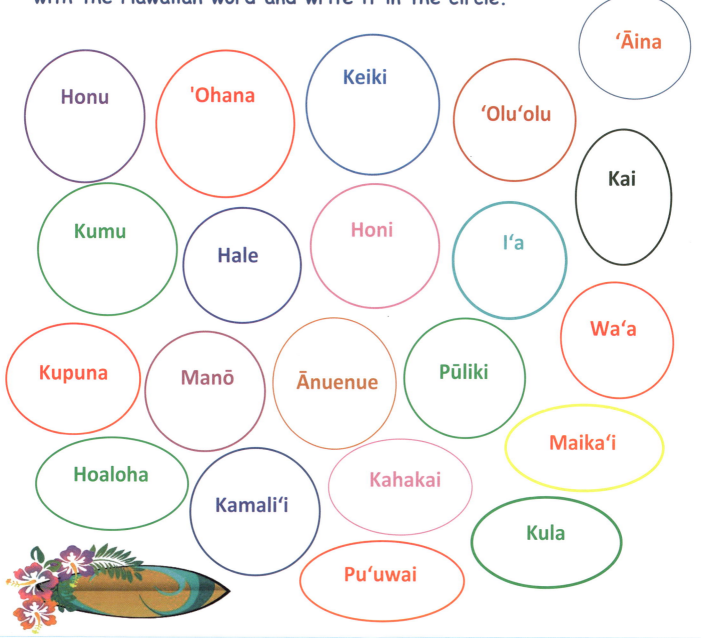

Hawaiian Language - Did you know??

*The Hawaiian language ('Ōlelo Hawai'i) is one of the oldest living languages in the world.

*When Hawai'i was annexed as a territory of the U.S. in 1891, the language was officially banned from the Government and schools, even at Kamehameha a private school for children of Hawaiian descent. The people were still allowed to speak Hawaiian and printed newspapers in their native language.

*Finally in 1978, the Hawaiian language was recognized as one of the official languages, along with English in the state of Hawai'i.

The Hawaiian alphabet

There are 5 vowels A, E, I, O, U and 8 consonants H, K, L, M, N, P & W (V)
An ' okina creates a pause like in "uh - oh". A kahakō (line over the o) creates an elongated Vowel sound.

A = "ah" like in alot   ā
E = "ey" or "ay" like in whey   ē
I = "ee" like in marine   ī
O = "o" like in older   ō
U = "oo" like in spoon   ū

Hawaiian Translation

Beach – kahakai
Breadfruit tree – 'ulu
Canoe - wa'a
Coconut - niu (nee-oo)
Conch shell - pū
Child - keiki (kay-kee)
Children - kamali'i
Elder - kupuna
Family - 'ohana
Fish - i'a
Flower - pua
Friend - hoaloha
Gift - makana
Good - maika'i (my-ee-kah'ee)
Hat - pāpale
Heart - pu'uwai
Help - kōkua
Honest - kūpono
House - hale
Hug - pūliki
Hungry - pōloli
Island – mokupuni
Kiss - honi
Land - 'āina

Learn - a'o
Life - ola
Love – aloha
Navigator - ho'okele wa'a
Nice - 'olu'olu
Ocean - kai
Peace - maluhia
Pineapple – hala kahiki
Prayer - pule
Rainbow - ānuenue (ah-noo-weh-noo-weh)
Responsibility - kuleana
Sacred site - heiau
School -- kula
Smile - mino'aka
Shark - manō
Star - hōkū (ho-koo)
Taro - kalo
Teacher - kumu
Thank You – mahalo (mah-hah-loh)
Thank You Very Much - mahalo nui
Trash - 'ōpala
Turtle - honu
Visitor – malihini
Work - hana

ALOHA is Love

Coupon Book

For: _____

ALOHA is Love

This Coupon is good for:

ALOHA is Love

This Coupon is good for:

ALOHA is Love

This Coupon is good for:

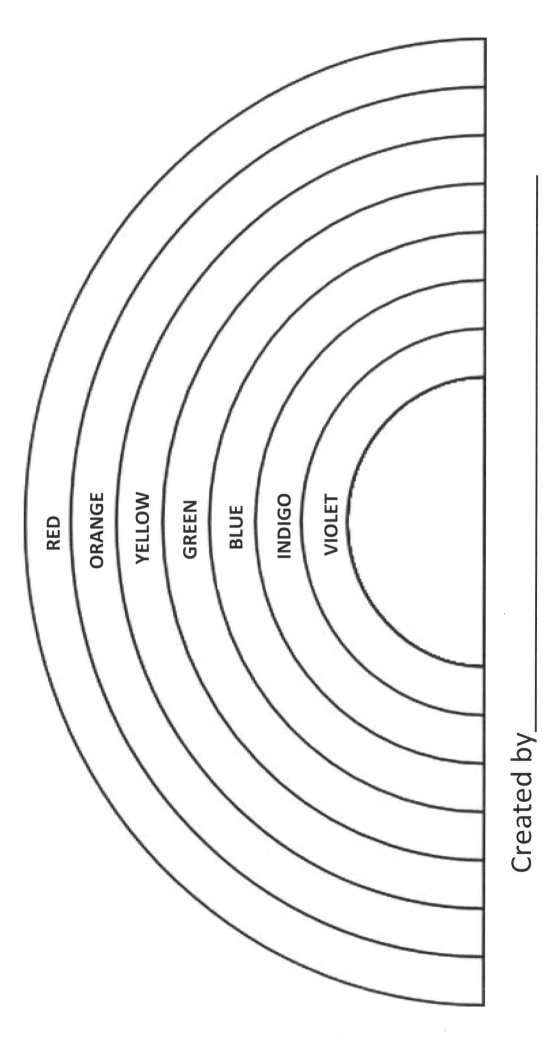

Created by _____

Rainbow Template for Aloha is Openness - Create a Rainbow Activity

Permission is given to remove this page, copy and then make your rainbow.

This activity can be done individually or with a hoaloah (friend).

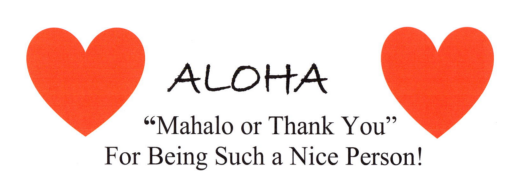

ALOHA
"Mahalo or Thank You"
For Being Such a Nice Person!

Kindness Wrappers - Cut out on the dotted lines after you copy the rainbow template. Instructions on Aloha is Kindness page.

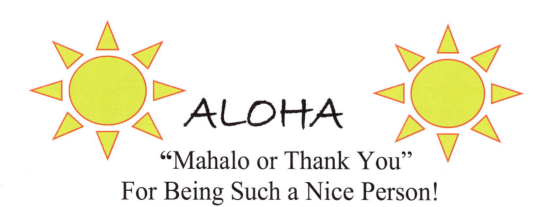

ALOHA
"Mahalo or Thank You"
For Being Such a Nice Person!